Norfolk Coast Sketches

by David Poole of Norwich

Wilson-Poole publishers

Acknowledgements

I am most grateful to the following people who loaned me photographs :—
Robert Malster of Ipswich, reporter and author.
John Hocknell, Eastern Daily Press photographer, King's Lynn.
David Cleveland, Audio Visual Centre, University of East Anglia.
Peter Stibbons of Lowestoft, schoolteacher and historian.
Mrs. Catling of Cley next to sea.
Edward and Stanley Craske of Sheringham.
Billy Bishop.
Basil Goffin, gamekeeper Holkham Estate.
Charles Darby and Gordon London.

I would also acknowledge with gratitude both Francis William Chandler of Holkham and Harry Dyer of Great Yarmouth. Both of these gentleman have died since the book was first published.

Norfolk Coast Sketches

First published   June 1980
Reprinted   May 1981 and September 1982
New Edition   May 1983

Repro by Photomation Graphic Arts, Norwich
Printed and bound in the United Kingdom by Page Bros (Norwich) Ltd.

Customs - House, Kings Lynn

3

King's Lynn is described elsewhere as being born of the strange and incomparable marriage of drowned misty and mysterious fens with high and dry windblown sandy heaths. Of the former, some feeling of atmosphere can be gained from such similar places that survive in the Broadland district of Norfolk. Examples of the latter still abound especially in Breckland.

Lynn is rich in history and bounded by unique regions. Charles I had great visions for the area including a new town to be called Charlemont, to absorb the increased market trade from the drained land. The design of the drainage was wisely given to a Dutch engineer, Vermuyden who together with later drainage supporters such as the Earl of Bedford and his Adventurers, succeeded in controlling both the vast volumes of sea-borne tidal water from the Wash and the river-borne rainwater. The cost has been astronomic.... but consider the land gained: The Great Level of the Fens, the hinterland of Kings Lynn, is 60 miles long by 30 miles wide. It covers 680,000 acres. Its soil is rich and black in colour. It has long been a highly productive region just right for the cultivator.

As for the Wash, there is nothing quite like it anywhere along England's coast: with its four Fenland rivers the Witham at Boston, the Welland northwest of Holbeach, the Nene north of Sutton Bridge, and the Great Ouse at Lynn, each broad, deep and slow emptying their waters into the vastness and mystery of this great North Sea bay: yellow with sandbanks in turn fissured by tidal streams and creeks. To men like Kenzie-Thorpe of Sutton Bridge a place of unbounded joy and freedom ...... having been a professional guide to ex-wildfowlers like Sir Peter Scott; but to others a sinister, secret place.

I have only stood at its edge and wondered as I peered across its vastness or wondered about going along to try to meet Kenzie-Thorpe as I drove through Sutton Bridge .... I have only walked some of its shoreline between Lynn and Thornham thus not knowing its fullness.

Fishermen washing down their vessel 'Kindly Light' as she rests on the bank of the River Ouse by Lynn.

Here again below is a sketch, a wash-drawing of the now abandoned quay with a delightful customs-house with its elaborate tower hinting at Wren churches, its dormers and the pitch of its roof at Inigo Jones domestic architecture; the date is 1683.

Not far away is the Tuesday marketplace bounded with fine graceful buildings; the Guildhall containing The Red Book of Lynn, the oldest paper book in existence; St. Margaret's in name memorial to a christian lady who preferred torture and death by beheading, rather than the betrayal of her Lord and God, Jesus Christ. Remarkably, the malicious torturer was a Roman general who desired her love but on his cruel terms. How very much all of us need the teaching of Jesus to help us to love ourselves and then our neighbours with his giving love. We are so naturally inclined to be selfish!

A drawing of the Fisher Fleet quay in the 1930's. There is still something of this atmosphere even though a more sound concrete quay has been made. One of the things that fascinate me is the size of the Great Ouse, its massive compared to the almost jumpable River Weasum in Norwich which is my most common yardstick. A small open ferryboat links the two halves of Lynn across the Ouse near the customs-house, the ferry being cheerfully handled by a big, well-made curly-headed ferryman — who I am glad to see carries a liberal supply of life-saving rings.

We have leap-frogged from Lynn over Hunstanton with its triple-coloured cliffs of white and red chalk and Carr stone and have swung eastwards away from the Wash to a place called Thornham. Now, the coast until Salthouse way, takes on a garment of compelling beauty, being a robe richly woven with the most beautiful threads, gleaming and glistening in the stark clear light: rivers and tidal creeks bounded with sea lavender and marramed dunes; desperate defence lines against the jealous unforgetful sea ...... these thin frail lines disguised with pine and grasses and shingle-banked in places ...... breached by the enormity of the mightier sea reclaiming its God-defined natural boundary; are consolidated in places like Scolt Head and Wells and Blakeney with sands and muds built up into islands and peninsulars.

Brancaster

A group of wood and brick sheds and stores where the mussel fishermen have their base.

In the background can be seen several of the village dwellings which sit either side of the coast road in linear fashion and extend along the road for a fair distance.

The creek alongside the sheds was quietly busy the last time I stopped by. One older man had rowed to the edge of the creek opposite a mud submerged timber fishing vessel with forlorn fingers reaching up along the rib lines black and stark. But the movement of the clean and bright dinghy rowed gently to the gorse-strewn bank attracted my attention, especially when the rower rested his oars and began talking with another old gentleman who leaned over and peered down to the dinghy and talked happily back. Nearby his contented dog sprawled half-sleeping on the path. Across the water two younger men were loading up another dinghy with sacks of shellfish. One had backed a trailer with the aid of a small tractor into about a foot of water and they began to load up the boat. Later, when the men were still talking of probably similar beautiful mornings decades ago, I saw the now heavily-laden dinghy with its oarsman pulling for all he was worth moving into the wider creek and heading towards Scolt Head and the mussel grounds.

The craft of the fisherman is often instilled into another at a very tender age. Here a father takes out his son upon the bright water.

Repairing a ship's rudder on the mud near
Scott Head, Brancaster.

Again, looking past the small ship under repair, the distant sand dune line is just discernible. The permanence of these dunes and ridges is largely set upon the growth of marram grass, sea blite, sea sandwort and many other plants, while man has assisted the natural process by planting such vegetation in especially vulnerable places.

There is a steady and natural reclamation of the lands within these protective coastal ridges that has formed the distinctive situations as here below at Scott and further east at Blakeney. Similarly, outside the natural defences and where no defences exist as at Stiffkey and Thornham, a similar process of consolidation is taking place. Each zone has its special flora, from the free-floating pelvetia seaweed and the zostera or wigeon grass of the tidal muds through the more solid areas where marsh samphire and sea aster flourish and this chain continues landwards through creeks fringed with sea purslane bordering land fully consolidated with a quilt of sea lavender, shrubby sea blite and various species of rushes and grasses.

Mussel fishermen, Brancaster preparing to go out to the mussel beds on the fast-flowing ebb tide. Three or four decades ago.

I spent five days in this beautiful, isolated village called Burnham Norton.
All the good richness of my life I owe to my Lord and friend Jesus. Through
the fellowship I mostly enjoy at Surrey Chapel, I met Meryl Sheen who
wrote from Wanigela, Papua New Guinea; where her husband Andy is helping
a local village community develop more upto date farming and boat-building
techniques..... and recommended I get in touch with her mother. So, in the
Summer of 1979 I telephoned Nora Moscrop and arranged to stay at "The Step"
for a few days in October.

Well the first thing I did when I arrived was to realise I was that much
nearer the North Pole and I looked imploringly at a very disinterested
wood-burning stove that smoked and did little else besides. Nora seemed to
enjoy being cold. I couldn't understand it. I'd forgotten my long johns
otherwise I would have leapt into those there and then.

That same afternoon, the lure of the saltings called to me and as warmly clothed as I considered necessary for the more open coast; I set off walking, passing an old lady with firewood under her arm and a curly-haired dog romping along beside her. (See page 16, Mrs. May Read). It wasn't long before I climbed over the relatively low grass-covered sea wall and onto the muddy saltings beyond. I waded across one pool which took my weight and then I began to cross another but this time I rapidly sank and water flooded into my boot. It is a treacherous place to the unknowing!
I spent a great deal of the time remaining roaming round the area, meeting local people and learning from them something of the area.... folk like John Taunton of Burnham Market, Laddy Lane of Burnham Overy, John and Victor Smith who have the farm by the water mill next to Burnham Overy Staithe and others further afield.

Mrs May Read whose late husband was a shepherd on Holkham Estate, lives in a terraced cottage opposite "The Step", Burnham Norton. Mrs. Read is a delicate being, over eighty years old but still capable of walking out three times each day to the marshes, accompanied by her beloved gingery brown curly-haired old dog. She possesses a gentleness, an almost dreamlike quality of peace and calm. She spoke warmly and charmingly of her late husband and of the kindness of the owners of Holkham Estate — which I understand own much of Burnham Norton.

Our village – Burnham Norton

Our village is a small one,
   But I would have you know,
A prettier spot you'll never find
   Wherever you may go.

Sunset o'er the marshes
   Sea lavender in bloom,
The tide when it comes flowing in,
   It's a lovely place to roam.

The cattle grazing contentedly
   The birds that soar above
They tell us of the many gifts,
   Sent from a God of love.

While the seasons come and go
   People come from far and wide,
To visit us and share with us,
   Our beauty spots and pride.

Time and tide will still go on
   When we come to the end
But we'll take a treasured memory
   As we journey to our friend.

         May Read

Before the Fens were reclaimed and drained there had been isolated "island" communities used to keeping sheep and cattle all the year round because they stored up good quantities of hay from the 'summer-dry' meadows. Elsewhere, along the northerly cap of Norfolk and in a broad band along the Peddar's Way there was a clear area of heathland which supported great numbers of sheep.

A great deal of Norfolk's rich heritage: the unique treasure of medieval churches, unequalled anywhere; was founded upon the wealth generated by the wool and weaving trade. These churches stand as 'Ebenezers' (rememberance stones) to God's provision and the responsiveness of a godly people who knew where to place their trust.

Now, in this largely Christless country we see the bitter fruits of a godless people: marriages breaking down, abortions, all manner of child cruelty .... but by God's grace the tide will turn and the love of Jesus will flood this barren land.

"The triangular island."

Two sketches of Burnham Overy Staithe : "Terns fishing in the creek."

I was staggered when I first saw
Burnham Overy several years ago and
it still overwhelms me with its pure
air and its clean beauty — especially
when Jenny and I took our daughters
Susan and Johanna for a picnic and
a paddle beyond the sand dunes. The
beach is usually, at most, occupied
by a couple of dozen people, some of
these preferring the shelter of the marram
clumps.
To see the meeting place of the creek
and the sea where the tide undercuts
the sand banks and they are almost
continuously flopping into the surging
water. I was surprised to discover that
I could wade across the outlet — the
water though raging was only knee-deep.
Oyster-catchers flashing white and
black with a touch of orange, fled when-
ever I drew close to their out-watchers.
Other waders swept into the air and
wheeled and banked, flashing like
dimmed signal lamps as they nervously
fled away to a temporarily safer
place. It felt like the edge of the
world.

On the opposite page : "Laddy Lane"
I warmly commend an exceptionally
fine book, "Fishermen" by Sally
Festing, in which can be found
accounts taken from conversations
with men of the coast like Laddy.
"Overy is finished. Young people
can't get houses to live in so they've
got to get out."
Laddy still potters about though
he retired in his late sixties.
When I saw him walking in the
deep grass at the foot of the sea-
wall, I never would have guessed
he was almost 83 years old.
The plain fact seems to be that
many people like Laddy have
enjoyed a combination of simple
good food, hard work and loads
of fresh air. Laddy is a jack
of all trades but is better known
for his expertise as a mussel —
fisherman, who has single-
mindedly endeavoured to protect
his mussel lays from careless
often plainly wicked lug-worm
diggers.

"the landlord of The Nelson public house". Nelson was
born nearby at Burnham Thorpe . Philip sat for me in
very trying light that streamed in through the window.
Yet he sat rock-still in spite of the discomfort.

"Ferrying visitors from the staithe at Burnham Overy"

20

21

Below is a drawing of "The Shipwright Arms, East Quay, Wells.
Firstly, I wish to remember one beautiful summer evening that Jenny
and I with our girls spent together with David and Judith Varvel and
their daughters, Nichola and Melanie. We had spent the afternoon at
Holkham Bay swimming and playing with the children. At teatime
we were treated to a most memorable picnic beautifully prepared by Judith.
By mid-evening we drove into Wells which by this time was bathed in
a glorious warm light from the westwards as the sun gently sank
into the horizon. We had a glass of beer and soft drinks for the children
and lingered by East Quay savouring the memorable moments of summertime.

Secondly, it is interesting and good to see Wells surviving as a lesser port. Once, together with Lynn, Blakeney and Yarmouth she shared the distinction of being as busy as an exporting port as all the rest of England, based on records of corn exported in 1795 and resulting from the effective Agricultural Revolution taking place especially in the nearby estate and elsewhere in Norfolk.

To the left of the Shipwright Arms and with smoke rising above it, is the whelk-boiling shed. Inside the shed one afternoon Alan Cox talked with me for a while: one thing he said stuck in my mind, "We never go to sea on a Sunday. Its a thing handed down from our fathers and their fathers. We just don't do it. If you can't earn your living in six days its a rummin!"

Burnham Overy Staithe, evening.

24

"Jack Cox, fisherman, lifeboatman and artist of Wells." One of the ways in which I have found help in developing as an artist has been to meet other artists; therefore having seen Jack's work in Norwich I wanted to go and meet with him and to learn from him what I could. Jack lives not far from the whelk sheds up the east end of Wells. His studio is by his vegetable plot roughly mid-way between home and the harbour. When I first met him one thing struck me forcibly above anything else, and that was the cruel state of his hands: they were cut and swollen and made far worse by the saltwater. At that time Jack was still fulltime fishing and of course his hands like all manual workers — told a tale or two. What staggered me was how on earth he managed to handle his paintbrush with such delicate effect. Nowadays, being days of retirement Jack finds far more time to paint. I believe he still gets up at a very early hour, lured by the unique beauty of the newly created day and at such times finds inspiration we late-risers miss. He has most often painted about Wells; not having a car his range though limited has gained by being umpteen times more intimate than fly-by-night artistry that endeavours to capture atmosphere in a flash. Jack's work as an artist has a fundamental honest accuracy and in spite of the restriction of travel I believe his work will be highly regarded for its skill and beauty. Jack showed me a large painting of Burnham Overy Staithe and in this he had gathered much of what he had learned over the years: a wonderful freedom of handling — there being little sign of hesitation; the use of a particularly pleasing golden light, not flooding the painting but thoughtfully combined with all the well drawn and composed elements that typify Burnham — especially the boats, which Jack having spent most of his life in, paints with thorough skill. Above all, I admire Jack for resisting the temptation to be "commercialised". He stands on his own two feet, his own man, a most gracious and strong man .... a most talented man!

"Cockling at Wells."

Looking westwards to the Shipwright Arms, Wells.

Holkham : the grounds are spacious, grand, generously patterned with trees gathered in woodlands, copses or smaller groups such as the Ilex evergreen oaks forming an avenue from the Obelisk to the South gates, have been open ever since the house was built 250 years ago. A large lake, wildfowl and a herd of wandering deer add to the fascinatingly natural feeling of the place...... helped by the grandeur of the Hall designed by Kent; stimulating a feeling of timelessness.

Viscount Coke, who manages the Estate, showed me a map representing the 25,000 acres...... it seems an immense place but it stands clearly on the daring, determined and diligent care of a growing idea..... to convert seemingly useless sand-covered land into highly productive acreage. Primarily, by marling — digging up underlying chalk and spreading it on the top, thickening and sweetening the topsoil. Turnips were grown, inspired by 'Turnip' Townsend of Raynham; sheep and cattle were added, increasing the fertility of the soil. Land was reclaimed from the sea and the new coastline strengthened with a rampart of fir trees. Gains and lessons learned were consolidated until we find the present-day situation: a stable and efficient place in a rapidly changing world.

Viscount Coke explained, "One very nice thing about living and working on an estate like this, is the sense of continuity. The estate role illustrates how families have maintained their links here from years back. Nearly all 300 dwellings on the estate have now been modernised. The tempting course of selling cottages to the holiday second-home market is avoided. Instead, we believe strongly in the encouragement and maintenance of village life, and to that end let houses only to local people." (see notes on Burnham Norton).

As Ironbridge in Shropshire is a focal point of the Industrial Revolution;

(continued page 30)

Viscount Coke — opposite

(cont. from p.28)
likewise, Holkham is a
jewel-like example of the
not so well appreciated
but vitally important
Agricultural Revolution
in the latter half of the
Eighteenth Century.

Two drawings of Basil Goffin, gamekeeper on
the estate. Bicycles with their handlebars hung
with rabbits were a common sight in the country
but the rabbit population has been heavily reduced
by recurring epidemics of myxomatosis. Basil,
like Harry Thain of West Somerton (see Broadland
Sketches) is an ex-steam trawlerman, and like
many people nowadays has had to adapt himself
as eras ended and new periods begin. He was
full of tales as I sat drawing him in the estate office;
giving out most entertaining and colourful stories
and accounts.

Ian Henry Whitworth, Agent for Viscount Coke.
"Running a large Estate fulfils my love of
preserving the English Heritage. My
particular interests are farming with
sheep (nothing gives me greater pleasure
than seeing the Shepherd with his sheep-
dog as the sun rises and the dew is still
on the ground); seeing young plantations
growing where there was once rough ground;
and living and working in a community where
those around me gain their livelihood from
the land. Some of the finest Farmers in
Norfolk are to be found on the Estate, and
there is always something to be learned on
every farm. In spite of keeping pace with
modern achievements, Holkham still remains
as a great monument to the past."

31

I am peacefully now and unashamedly a creationist, simply believing, and that belief a precious free gift of God, in the sure knowledge that God is a God of infinite love, far exceeding our understanding, measurement or experience.

I believe God in his inestimable love for us, decided to give his only son, Jesus that by his perfect life he would firstly demonstrate vividly, abundantly and supernaturally how we might live in true spiritual worship of God – enjoying, yes! actually enjoying this life to its fullest measure.

Oh lamentably, we have too readily disagreed with God's way, and our lives have been empty of the very love that is uppermostly honoured by God.

If you wonder about this love: there is no need to be puzzled anymore for the creative force of God who is Spirit, 'dared' to reveal himself in human form; boldly was born yet conceived supernaturally by the very Holy Spirit; grew in his earthly mother's virgin womb, undefiled and unassailed by any aborter's hand. was born and briefly worshipped wondrously by wise kings and angel-urged shepherds; grew as a boy child and when only twelve enthralled doctors of his nation's intricate but man-elaborated law, with his clear intuitive grasp of it.

Amazingly, amazingly Jesus waited; what obedient patience he exercised in this triple-decade lifespan.

"Then a voice was heard crying out from the wilderness. A magnetic, enthralling sound so designed by God that the people flocked to this prophetic man. "John's clothes were made of camel's hair, and he had a leather belt around his waist. His food was locusts and wild honey. People went out to him from Jerusalem and all Judea and the whole region of the Jordan. Confessing their sins, they were baptised by him in the Jordan River."

He had some strong things to say of the religious people of his day, people more concerned with form and ceremony than with life of truth and spirit. "You brood of vipers! Who warned you to flee from the coming wrath. Produce fruit in keeping with repentance."

John continued no doubt astonishing, appalling those he addressed for he was so utterly different from them, "I baptise you with water for repentance. But after me will come one who is more powerful than I, whose sandals I am not fit to carry. He will baptise you with the Holy Spirit and fire."

"Then Jesus came from Galilee to the Jordan to be baptised by John. But John tried to deter him, saying, 'I need to be baptised by you, and do you come to me?'"

"Jesus replied, 'Let it be so now; it is proper for us to do this to fulfil all righteousness.' Then John consented.

"As soon as Jesus was baptised, he went up out of the water. At that moment heaven was opened, and he saw the Spirit of God descending like a dove and lighting on him. And a voice from heaven said, 'This is my Son, whom I love; with him I am well pleased.'"

Two things stand out from the word of God written above, the first being that incontestably there is no benefit in anything other than true repentance and a submission to the baptism by the Holy Spirit and by immersion in water as a believer in Jesus as Lord.

We need to get right with God, this is true repentance. If we move in this way God will draw us to Jesus. (A wonderful truth, God moves us by grace to his son — his love).

Now, don't be afraid that you are somehow unusual. Remember Jesus came to save us and not to condemn us. Just be totally honest and God will give you peace .... he promises and does lift from us the grim burden of guilt. No matter what wrong/s we have committed.

Secondly, the great news is that Jesus came that we might have NEW LIFE, life in all its fulness. Being the most outstanding teacher of all, his instructions were backed up by practical demonstrations that left his followers and especially those willing to learn, in no doubt that his way, his life was utterly different. His dependance upon God his father was total — no wonder then his Father poured out all heavenly gifts into his life.

Now again, dont let anyone persuade you against the truth. LOOK FOR YOURSELF. Search and you will find. Go where the truth of God and the life of Jesus is being lived in this day in which we are living.

Don't get into the religious habit of saying or tolerating "But we cant have ......" Because the truth is that God has said 'His divine power has given us everything we need for life and godliness.'
(and the Scripture cannot be broken)

Morston Creek

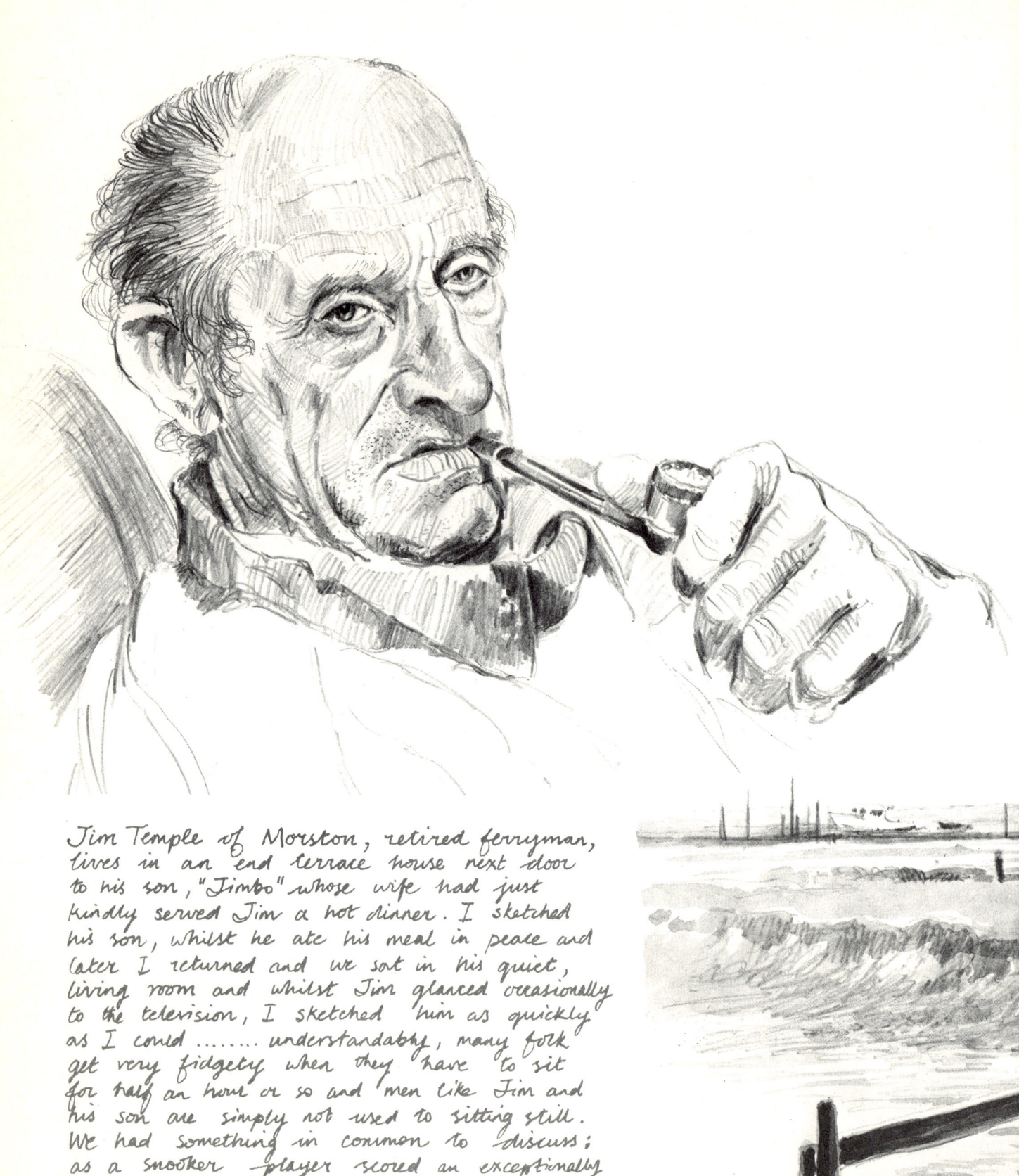

Jim Temple of Morston, retired ferryman, lives in an end terrace house next door to his son, "Jimbo" whose wife had just kindly served Jim a hot dinner. I sketched his son, whilst he ate his meal in peace and later I returned and we sat in his quiet, living room and whilst Jim glanced occasionally to the television, I sketched him as quickly as I could .... understandably, many folk get very fidgety when they have to sit for half an hour or so and men like Jim and his son are simply not used to sitting still. We had something in common to discuss; as a snooker player scored an exceptionally high break on Pot Black, so time passed happily enough within the fascinating atmosphere of Jim's cottage.

The warden of Blakeney Point, Ted Eales lives in Morston but he was away on the two occasions I called.

One day in February I called at Morston again and found Jim outside his cottage on a triangle of sodden grass that was covered with a small tractor, tarpaulin – protected from the rain; there were various attachment components nearby and a large pile of timber and logs.

Jim proudly showed me the freshly-painted small tractor, "All my life I've wanted a tractor like this, now I'm as happy as a sandboy, that I am! Look, its even got a plough and a small harrow and a box. Then there's this pulley attachment that can drive that there saw. Yus, I've allus wanted a tractor like this 'ne."

(That same day yet another man was to express similar happiness with his lot).

That day in February found the lane down to the creek heavily waterlogged, but there isn't much activity in the winter, leastways from the ferryman's point of view. Jim's son was a few miles away cutting reed at Cley with Bernard Bishop, but now in retirement, Jim could potter away to his heart's content readying the beloved, versatile machine for the coming times of usefulness .... his quiet life being occasionally punctuated by boilers exploding in nearby houses — a singular incident in fact, that gave Jim a bit of a fright as the roof was blasted off above the kitchen — there was no fire and nobody was hurt as the owners were away at the time.

It was perishing weather damp and deeply cold as I left Jim in the fine rain outside his cottage absorbed in his dreams for the coming days, surrounded by the substance of one long-held dream.

One of the picturesque footbridges at Morston.

At one time the populations of coastal communities from the Wash right round the Norfolk bulge to the Thames estuary lived largely on or from the sea. Life in them was close-knit and parochial, and each village had its own identity. It was a rough life they led but there were many whose principles were strict enough. The spirit of sacrifice showed itself time and again in rescue operations and as the majority of them were religious, when the Salvation Army began its work, many flocked to it.

Large families brought together under constant threat of sudden bereavements shared one another's prolonged sorrows and brief joys. There is no mistaking that they live as they are, without any attempt at pretension or disguise. Life for them must be taken as it comes with all its paradoxes. And not least of their attractions is a readiness to experience realities. Often it is the trivial, the chance remark that reveals this attitude, an unconscious yearning to plummet back to the fount of things. They feel, sometimes without the means to express themselves, that counterfeit happenings tend to drive out spontaneous enjoyment of what is real, what finally matters.

Blakeney and Cley were bustling with wool exports when Liverpool and Southampton were scarcely known. In fact it was this trade using North Norfolk ports, that earned her town's prosperous churches by the 14th and and 15th centuries. Sally Festing's 'Fishermen'.

below : A sailing vessel in the harbour. (notice the donkey cart in the foreground).

"Jimbo" Temple the Morston ferryman. Boatload after boatload of children and grown-ups carried from the creek quay-heading to the bird sanctuary of Blakeney Point; transported in wide-beamed clinker-built boats that surge along the tidal channel and across The Pit to the clean sands with their colony of terns on the sandy peninsular that has for many years fascinated visitors with its isolated beauty.

Jimmy Long and his greyhound taken from an old bromide in the late Peter Catling photographic collection.

Jimmy and Annie Rooney with their daughter at Cley, 1910.
This family earned their living begging and singing in public houses.

Blakeney harbour at the west end in the nineteenth century,
nowadays nearby, there stands a beautiful low-lying building
called or referred to as an eighteenth century farmhouse
in Doreen Wallace's 'East Anglia'. Some of the many beech
trees that sheltered it are still standing although it is
less conspicuous since the front wall has been built up.

Old Blakeney Bridge

Old George Long : two glimpses of a
fine character from the past. Once he
would have been as well known about Blakeney
as presently, John Wallace deserves to be.
George was the coxswain of the lifeboat and
also, probably in his 'retirement' earned a
little income as a waterman.
Below we see him in a very confident
mood having been contentedly stewing
up cockles on Blakeney Point.

opposite page : Barnacle geese heading
out from near Bacton.

40

42

above, looking across The Pit to Blakeney Point at sundown.

on the opposite page, Blakeney Harbour when it was able to take trading vessels circa 1900. In the foreground 'Admiral Mitford', then in order behind, 'Clam', 'Pioneer', 'Tigress', 'Lion' and 'Yankee'.

In spite of the death of Blakeney as a trading port, it survives as a lively sailing centre and even the addition of a hotel on the harbour front has not been such a bad thing for it has been designed and built very beautifully to blend in sympathetically with its scene-sisters.

Yes, in spite of the change, this ghost harbour of the North Coast has a most attractive atmosphere, especially out of season.

Again a leap backalong the coast and to Blakeney Quay.

This place can be so peaceful as when my wife, Jenny and I stayed at the hotel one weekend in the early springtime. On the first morning we were over—whelmed at the beauty we saw. The tide had crept in and quietly spilled over the saltings and the quay. As we looked out and later as we walked by the creek the dawnlight was mirrored in thousands of tidal pools across the saltings; and strongly, the sun gleamed on the waters of the creek. Far away geese restless with migratory fever were getting up in smaller flights and flying about The Pit and towards The Point.

In contrast and about Autumntime the tidal waters spill over the quay once more and Blakeney holds a sort of carnival or water frolic with fair, greasy pole and all.

I close with a few notes about another man I admire for his single-minded care of his environment: a chap called John Wallace of Beacon Cottage, Blakeney. When I called on him, John invited me in and guided me up the narrow hallway assuring me that the small wiry-haired brown dog on a string would not harm me. He led the way into a spacious but carefully-cluttered room filled with interest: books, paintings, a room that was comfortable but purposeful with shallow drawer chests and shelves of interesting ornaments and personalia.

At one end was a huge oak-beamed open fireplace with a cooking cauldron - disused. The oak beam carried guild marks or trade signs similar to these: indicating the possibility that the room or house had been a meeting place for the local guildsmen.

John is amazed at the vandalism of our day but especially at the attitude of adults: he told me of a man and a young boy who he found in the act of stealing an anchor, who said when John challenged him:

"Well, I wanted a genuine antique one".

"If you take it the boat will drift off; you can't do that!" John said. "What's it got to do with you. I'll do what I like," replied the man. You might find it strange but I see the same kind of careless disregard for the resultant effect in the greedy acquirement of holiday homes — particularly those who live perhaps only 3 or 4 weeks in a year in such a place. They make ghouls, empty heartless places of such earlier lively properties and contribute a 'respectable' vile decay to the area.

45

Thalatta.

Howard Brett of Cley, three studies of a man
who had responsibility for the Rocket Brigade
using the apparatus invented by Captain Manby
of Great Yarmouth. Mr. Brett also fished and
applied himself to other interests. In the middle
study he proudly wears two medals won for
rescue work, using the rocket-fired lifelines
that crossed the tantalisingly short distance from
ship to shore, that carried life to otherwise certain death.

47

two studies of the legendary :
Billy Bishop retired warden of Cley
reserve after 42 years faithful service.
(see further notes page 51.)

Billy's son,
Bernard Bishop who
is the present warden.

One beautiful morning I encountered amidst the serenity of the Morston saltmarshes, its tidal creek and Blakeney Pit the quiet industry of the two men sketched below as they went about the business of netting whitebait on the ebb tide.

Sailing lighters in Cley harbour at the turn of the century.

below: the grim results of man's indifference, his carelessness towards other living creatures — wildfowl drowned or suffocated in crude oil and flung upon the beaches.

Cley windmill, a great sentinel by the sea. I jotted down some basic thoughts from Billy Bishop: priority number one for any warden — knowledge of habitat. Knowing what the birds want. He estimated that one stoat could kill off 365 birds each year; therefore it was vitally necessary to control the 4-footed aggressors such as stoats and rats, also carrion crows and the occasional rogue black-headed gull. He remembers seeing a godwit hanging over something: the male had just been killed in the nest. Within three hours Billy had trapped and destroyed the stoat ..... this then allowed the female to hatch and rear four more godwits. Its really good to see how the Norfolk Naturalist Trust has kept its pledge made to Billy by Dr. Long over 40 years ago, 'You look after us Billy and we will take care of you.' There is now a beautiful new house with a most contented and retired Mr. & Mrs. Billy Bishop living in it next to their son's "Watcher's Cottage", Cley.

Joe Jordan, spear-fishing at Stiffkey (see page 55)

Derek Osborne, Vicar of St Peter and St Paul the 14th century church of Cromer. I had been lay-preaching at Mundesley and together with the family and three friends Margaret Manning, Chris Le Breton and Andy Reid we drove to Cromer the same Sunday evening to take part in a Sing-a-long service of worship in the great church. Derek is greatly gifted by God to convey the joy of Jesus, the simply lovely atmosphere of shared praise and worship is well worth experiencing within the grandeur of this house of God.

Salthouse sketched from the heath above the village. The church looks like a fortress and was wisely built on higher ground. This village shares with many other settlements on the East Coast the real fear of invasion by the sea. The church in this regard is safe but several cottages adjacent to the coast road have been and continue to be threatened by any breaching by the sea of the remarkably rudimentary shingle bank sea-wall.

Last year in connection with Ted Ellis's book, 'Countryside Reflections' I visited Kelling Heath near Sheringham in order to illustrate one of the beautiful poems, 'Thorn on the Heath'. Of its kind it is a mini-paradise environmentally: not readily inviting to the visitor thus it is often extremely lonely and this aids peaceful contemplation. Ted lyrically conveys this with such lines as :—

The thorn is dark up on the heath
 This winter day
And the hill is crowned with a red fern wreath,
 Raggedly gay.
The sun is silvered in a cloud ;
 The wind is chill
And woods are wrapt in a sea-mist cloud
 By Weybourne Mill.

         Ted Ellis.

A drawing from a press photograph taken in 1966 and entitled, "The Old Men of the Sea".

From left to right Teddy "Fiddy" West, Bob "Joyful" West, Jimmy "Paris" West and sitting Henry "Joyful" West At the time they were in attendance at an exhibition of photographs displayed in the old lifeboat shed at the West End slipway housing the sailing-and-oars boat, then 72 years old and which they had all crewed in, the Henry Ramey Upcher. According to Jimmy "Teapot" West who I sketched very recently in Norwich the new lifeboat station at Sheringham is not as straightfoward to use and indeed I watched the modern lifeboat being re-stationed utilising turntable and tractor – it certainly looked an awkward job.

LIFEBOAT ROCK 1/=

55

Launching a crab boat in days of lug sail and oars, when these boats were not so heavily built as those today carrying engines. Nontheless, the perils of the sea were close at hand. This phase of the fisherman's work is the most dangerous for it is most difficult to launch boats against an oncoming wind and requires masterly timing to bring them up the steeply sloping shelving beaches. Two Cromer boats were caught by a sudden gale only fifty yards off shore and dashed to pieces and seven men in them drowned, on one occasion. Lifeboats have always made a significant proportion of their rescues to the local fishing fleet.

Two Sherringham fishermen in the
days when they wore knitted garnseys
that were individually-patterned.
Fishermen from this village are known
as "Shannocks".
There is a strong sense of history in the
area ..... of the days when sleek longships
disgorged fierce sea raiders called Vikings,
who were a maritime explosive force — especially in the 9th. and 10th. centuries; who
here and there after raiding, settled as in Norfolk.

Edward 'Teddy' Craske of Sheringham. His name was given to me
by the equally famous West family one of whom, Henry "Joyful" West
is the present coxswain of the Sheringham lifeboat.
I was surprised to learn how 'Teddy' had agreed to come out of his
retirement to teach a young nephew, one of the West family the fishing
art. 'Teddy' is over seventy and wisely does the teaching outside
the more cruel and dangerous winter season.
I realise there are more well known lifeboatmen than 'Teddy' Craske
but I felt led to shine a little light on the not so well known crew
members....... who nontheless travel the same wickedly wily waves as

their coxswains. On the left is a
sketch of 'Teddy' carrying a wounded
merchant seaman ashore from the
lifeboat during the Second World War.
The Heinkel 111 responsible for the
machine gunning of this and other
seamen and the sinking of the ship
is seen on page 60, itself having
been shot down by spitfires. The
surprising thing being that the three
German airmen escaped uninjured
from the air battle, though of
course were later captured by the
local Home Guard near Cley.
(I'm fairly sure Captain Mainnering
was not the officer in charge).
Jimmy 'Paris' West in Sally Festing's,
"Fishermen": "That first mile off the coast
is the worst and the first half mile is
treacherous. To get clear of the shore, the
breakers where they hit over the beach is
everybody's fear and that's what we have
to go through each day when we're
doing our job. That was the reason the
lifeboat had to come off so many times."

'Were there always two broad types of fishing people, the principled and the rip-roaring'? Certainly not all were true to the popular pattern of hard-swearing, hard-drinking old reprobates.

For instance, the Sheringham fishermen who settled in Grimsby helped to build the Citadel in Duncombe Street — they sawed the wood and carved the pulpit and pews themselves, and at one period the Grimsby lifeboat crew was almost solidly Salvationist and Shannock. The Rushmers came from this kind of background.'

"All my people were Methodists and I still am. Even today there are fishermen who won't go to sea on a Sunday but they never used to go however bad the catch had been during the week. There'd be a few rough ones, but by and large, they were a God-fearing race. John 'Teapot' West and Willy Long were Evangelists and the chapel in Station Road was called Fishermen's Chapel because the preachers and most of the congregation were fishermen. They were very strict, good-living, Bible-reading people. I think it was the hardships they encountered daily and the things you see at sea, well the landsman has no knowledge of them. It's as the Psalm 107 says": Sally Festing's 'Fishermen'.

verse 23. They that go down to the sea in ships
that do business in great waters;

24. These see the works of the Lord,
and his wonders in the deep.

25. For he commandeth, and raiseth the stormy wind,
which lifteth up the waves thereof.

26. They mount up to the heaven, they go down again to the depths:
their soul is melted because of trouble.

27. They reel to and fro, and stagger like a drunken man,
and are at their wits' end.

28. Then they cry unto the Lord in their trouble,
and he bringeth them out of their distresses.

opposite page : Sheringham

Heinkel III shot down by Spitfires near Cley in the Second World War

Three Cromer fishermen in the early part of this century. They look like Old Testament prophets with their straight, clear-eyed gazing out from treasured old photographs. The man, above right belonged to the Rooke family, who can trace their ancestors back through Cromer fishermen to the 16th century.

A lifeboat has always held a great deal of interest and to the left is a carriage-launch from the beach, showing men endeavouring to move the awkward carriage nearer to the sea; with the crew aboard optimistically waiting to unship oars and cross the difficult breakers.

63

Victorian Cromer

Edwardian Cromer

Cromer beach today. Very much more casual than in the days of formal dress and bathing machines that allowed the proper, relatively hidden transition from beach to briny. Though once the over-dressed madams were in to the water, they were well and truly exposed to the cool waters of the North Sea and the not surprising scrutiny from the shore. It must have been like a circus! Nowadays, things are so much calmer and more normal on the beaches hereabouts. In spite of its popularity the beach at Cromer is still roomy even in the high season; being nothing like as crowded as Great Yarmouth's broad beach.

It's good to see older folk enjoying the beach and contemplating a paddle.

Winterton church from inland: I sketched this on a bitterly cold winter's day, resting my sketchboard on the top of the car to steady my hands.

The fishermen's cottages, Scratby; three older folk gazing out to sea from the cliffs.

Walcot - on - Sea in the 1930's.

On the following two pages, 72 and 73 are ten drawings that I prepared about nine years ago for a book called, "When will it be Morningtime". It seems remarkable that nine years have passed and less remarkable that I have still to pull that title together. I was advised to send a chapter or two to a publisher but this only brought a most puzzling rebuff about it being too personal .... this book is about the short but significant life of our only son, Simon who died in August, 1970 of leukaemia. I believe that the healing love of Jesus has wrought a miracle in my life in this regard — that I have never felt any bitterness in my mind and heart over losing Simon. Jenny and I grieved, we grieved and wept together many, many times for a good year afterwards and then slowly the painful agony ebbed away and his memory softened and the vivid cruel images and memories of sounds and so on dissolved and in their turn, they too died away.

There'ore, I firmly believe that it would be right to begin soon to complete the book and to answer the question our little boy asked in the long painful, fearful nights — 'Daddy or Mummy, when will it be morningtime?' Yes indeed, when will such suffering cease to have to be? That and other relevant and contentious eternal questions I, like many others, many other bereaved parents have asked and have searched for a satisfactory reply. And in looking more carefully and faithfully at Jesus I am beginning to understand the mystery and to see God's answer to parents and to all mankind, to all suffering mankind.

"Come to me, all you who are troubled, fearful, and I will give you rest."

Ten sketches of Scratby 1971

Mr Edmunds' old dog that he allowed us to take for a walk along the cliffs towards Hemsby.

Looking backalong the road towards the Post Office.

Beach View Farm, red brick, black painted linters and green woodwork and rainwater pipes. The propped christmas tree by the door still stands. Sadly, Mrs. Edmunds has passed away and Mr Edmunds has sold the site and moved away.

Mrs. Fitzgibbon's caravan. It was a bit like packing sardines into a can but it gave Jenny and Simon and I a much needed break. How beautifully the Edmunds kept the site — they took a great pride in the place. It was a quiet and very restful situation that did much to strengthen us for future days.

at left, Hemsby – bungalows in the dunes.

The pigeon loft against the barn at Beach View Farm, and other small outbuildings. The pigeons added to the tranquil quality of the place and I have always enjoyed watching such birds since my boyhood when in Sale Park we would rather mischievously follow them about until their patience ran out and they took to flight with noisy wingbeat.

outbuildings at Beach View farm.

Studies of several of the pigeons.

Pigeons at
Beach Road Farm.

The old Post Office, its gone now but it was filled with a clutter of interest, especially for children.

I was surprised and thrilled to see that this, the entrance to Beach View Farm caravan site is relatively unchanged.

The back of the fishermen's cottages, Scratby, see page 70. A fine combination of pantiles, Norfolk Reds, flints and beach stones with rusting iron guttering and old rickety gates.

73

The coastline of Norfolk is full of surprises and here at Winterton it again amazed me by the width of the sand dune area between the village and the beach. I climbed up the remains of what might have been a Beach Company lookout post that stood prominently in the middle of the duned area. I could see, even from its reduced height far out to sea but now the sea was empty: empty of herring, empty of those thousands upon thousands of carefully carved and adzed fishing and trading vessels. In years gone by catches of immature fish were tolerated, catches that included immature herrings so small that 35 would fit in a matchbox. Spring herring were caught further limiting breeding. Where have the herring gone? The old men stare out to sea and recall those great, grim and short-sighted days. Yet I have some inkling of the struggle we have as human beings to sacrifice today for tomorrow or next year's good. To give up something whilst others around are indifferent to any higher levels of thinking than the widespread: 'grab what you can, while you can' that cripples our civilisation which is like a rotten pie with a hard crust.

grey plover

redshank

immature herring gulls.

curlew sandpiper

heron

gadwall

curlew

Shag

pintail

guillemot

'Fifteen studies' Ian Wallace

Young herring gull.

Red breasted goose

Canada

W. J. Rudd aged 74 who kindly allowed me to sketch him very quickly
as he patiently and carefully looked out to sea from the Winterton coastguard
station. Mr. Rudd was a skipper on a fishing vessel at 24.

David Poll 1977

These three spritsail barges which I sketched in all truth in an inland port called Maldon on the Blackwater, Essex, remind me of two things. Firstly, the way the flat mud of Breydon up the Yarmouth end not far from Vauxhall Station was used for the mooring of such vessels as these which were designed to settle down upon relatively smooth and level stretches of tidal mudflats like wooden whales marooned in between tides.

Secondly, the thrilling account of the Cromer lifeboat H.F. Bailey, under the command of Henry Blogg, which describes the rescue of the skipper and mate from the sinking sailing barge, Sepoy, wrecked off Cromer. I recommend the book by Cyril Jolly, "Henry Blogg of Cromer" in which this rescue is recorded.

Within 200 yards of the shore the bucking and heaving sailing barge, with its two crewmen clinging for their lives, was being ground and broken upon the sea bottom by ice cold surging seas driven by wild winds from the East.

4 rocket lines were fired, one actually laying across the stern of the Sepoy, but the second Cromer lifeboat, 'Alexandra' passed by shortly after the line was secured to rigging, and parted the rope. Shortly after this the Alexandra was flung onto the beach for the third time. (She was a pulling — oar and sail lifeboat). Meanwhile the motor-driven H.F. Bailey under Blogg had heard of Sepoy's plight and sped back from near Yarmouth after tending another sailing barge that had been wrecked called 'Glenway'. Blogg and his crew came back through seas as bad as they had ever previously experienced; often shipping 'green', the men had to be cheered with a tot of rum from the emergency ration cupboard — though typically Blogg took none himself. So they finally battled back to Cromer and the savagely battered Sepoy (cont.)

Jack Cates of Norwich, the last trading skipper of the wherry, Albion. Albion is owned by the Norfolk Wherry Trust. She is a black-sailed trader — a beautiful sight about the Broads. This type of vessel was similar in use to the sailing lighters of Blakeney and Cley; in that she and others sailed out to the Yarmouth Roads and unloaded vessels off shore, then brought their cargoes into the intricate system of inland waterways.

(continued from page 79)
The rescue had to take place in the most hazardous area of the sea — in shore. Blogg after three orthodox attempts had failed, drove in from the lee side of the barge and actually set the lifeboat on the bulwarks, the deck of the barge close to the rigging. Quickly, the mate John Stevenson of Grays, Essex was rescued but agonisingly, Captain Hemstead had to wait yet again for the lifeboat was swept off Sepoy by a large wave. Blogg came back again, the captain was rescued and finally the damaged but victorious H.F. Bailey and her crew with the saved seamen were safely guided ashore into the willing arms of men like Tom "Bussey" Allen who had been soaked 3 times that day with the Alexandra.

There is something deeply extraordinary about the risking of one's life for a complete stranger. Henry Blogg was disgusted by a friend who was reluctant to get his shoes wet and who stopped at the edge of the sea. Blogg simply explained to this friend after tearing him off a strip, "I go because they need me".
It's crazy from some points of view like a wreck itself..... often unapproachable from many points of the compass — but there is a way and that's why this often obscure, precious way of the salvation of souls in distress at sea is so singular. It seems to bottom to truly plumb to the very heart of mankind...... it causes the emotions to be stirred by the universal language of man's too infrequent sacrificial devotion to his brother's safety and wellbeing.
These lifeboatmen, in this especial way, are their brothers keepers. They rise to the pinnacle of human caring; undeterred by any foreignness of those in peril, and no wonder we shorebound watchers are overwhelmed by their great courage.

opposite page : A steam drifter by Gorleston.

Jetties by the River Bure
at confluence with the River
Yare at Great Yarmouth.

below: the harbour at Yarmouth
silos, cranes and rig-service
vessels of all shapes and sizes.

David Ferrow, antiquarian bookseller of Great Yarmouth. His shop
quite near Haven Bridge is a fascinating one filled with a wide range
of books, especially on marine subjects and local subjects.

There are times when suddenly we take stock, contemplating the nature of our existence, ruminating and considering just what life is all about. For some perhaps its easier to do this but indisputably we all have the freedom to choose to consider the quality and nature of our existence and to effect a change, should we conclude it necessary.

In the recently published book, 'Living from the Sea' by David Butcher there is an interesting conclusion following a rich variety of personal testimonies of both fishermen and farmworkers. The gist of it is that in the 'dazzlingly fast rate' of technical discovery there has been a very heavy price paid indeed. Man who came from and who is deeply connected to the very dust of the earth, a groundsman, a landsman irrevocably, is often dismayed and unconvinced that so-called technological advances are always beneficial to him.

Technology at worst is so hard and mechanical, so indifferent intrinsically to tiny, by comparison, personal needs of mere human beings. 'Scientific indigestion' is the term the above author uses, more to the point for many less-educated, less-intrigued with all this nonsense people, are not so much in a state of indigestion as estrangement. And no where more than in ancient settlements, villages and towns that have lost their communal hearts; for example the country villages and coastal towns.

You cannot turn the clock back its true, but what is happening as we become more thoughtful of and less dismissive of the past is that we can begin to see the very real value of a community. In a village whose inhabitants largely lend their lives, their labour to the sea or to the land, it is easier

to nurture and maintain this invaluable quality of community.
Adversity has some redeeming aspects, not least the tendency to
provide the opportunity for helping others or, in turn and probably
more difficult, receiving help from other neighbours within the
community.

In both my limited knowledge and experience I have never dis-
covered anything more precious than the community model and
instructions for its perfect functioning, found in the Book of
Acts, the New Testament part of the bible. What is being shown
here is that despite all that the oppression, of either a tyrannical
ruler or a technologically indifferent system, can depress life:
in spite of this God has designed and made available to all
of us a community which is so able to conquer the problems
such as considered hithertofore.

This community is so wonderful for it is boundless and ageless; it is
vibrant, ever increasing as it is filled with the love, the power
and the knowledge of God. It is the abundant life Jesus promised.

I was reading 'The Woodlanders' a novel by Thomas Hardy and there is an interesting description of an old horse that reminds me of those I sometimes see at Great Yarmouth: "The old horse, whose hair was of the roughness and colour of heather, whose leg-joints, shoulders and hoofs were distorted by harness and drudgery from colthood — though if all had their rights he ought, symmetrical in outline, to have been picking the herbage of some Eastern plain instead of tugging here — had trodden this road daily for almost twenty years. Even his subjection was not made congruous throughout, for, the harness being too short, his tail was not drawn through the crupper, and the breeching slipped awkwardly to one side."

I cannot speak with authority about the employment of horses but I am sure they prefer to be challenged by work than to stand about small fields looking extremely forlorn. There is work and work and compared to the quoted example which dealt with a horse drawn passenger carrying van, the landaus of the type illustrated below are probably not so heavy.

When I was a boy one of the fascinations of the streets where I lived was sight, sound and smell created by the horses pulling various roundsman's carts : coal, baker's, rag and bone. From giant Shires their nostrils smoking like dragons on a frosty morning to bad-tempered, biting ponies pulling even worse-tempered old drivers, calling out : 'Any old rags, any old rags!' Steaming bodies, pungent leather, nose bags of oats, urine and dung; the striking sound of iron shod great feet upon the roads and cobbled entries, enrichened our childhood as indeed these carriages lend a fascination to the
promenade.

87

1913 was the zenith of both steam vessels and the British fishing industry. For half a century the industry had grown vigourously and 1913 saw a year in which the record catch of herring reached half a million tons. But this represented only a half of the total of fish caught. The trawler fleets, largely made up of steam vessels were landing huge catches of cod, plaice and other bottom feeding fish from the still prolific fishing grounds of the North Sea and beyond.

This was a time when, remarkably, you would actually walk across the Yare by the decks of hundreds of drifters that packed the harbour.

But 1913 was a turning point. In less than a year the celebrations over huge catches had ended and the crews had traded in red ensigns for white ensigns and were soon fishing for mines during the First World War.

Their world rapidly dwindled. It must have been heart – breaking to many, to men like Harry Train, W. J. Rudd and Basil Goffin and hundreds of others...... bewildered to see their proud steam vessels that had been so right technically and seaworthily, running quickly into obsolescence.

Ironically, Yarmouth harbour has been emptied of the very last of these: the sailing drifter Lydia Eva which sailed for London last year. Whilst some small inshore fishing boats can be seen at Darby's Hard and elsewhere at Yarmouth, only nearby Lowestoft owns the nearest and significant though small fleet of modern vessels.

In The East Anglia Film Archive housed in the University of East Anglia under the loving care of Malcolm Fregard and David Cleveland, I was shown a 1928 film of "Fishing on the Dogger Bank". The vessels were steam drifters with thin, tall smoke stacks that caused the name, 'Woodbine Willies' to be coined.

But what impressed itself upon my mind as David ran the film through was the nature of the North Sea way out there by the Dogger Bank and the working conditions on the vessels.

The film concentrated on an exercise called 'Fleeting', similar to the employment of a central factory ship which is large enough to absorb the catches from many smaller fishing vessels. Initially the system demanded that fishermen loaded their catch into trays and then into tenders whence they were rowed oftentimes precariously, over the lively sea to the collecting vessel. Glued to my seat I watched as they came alongside and made fast. As many as half a dozen rowing boats gathered in a clutch at the ship's side and rose not simultaneously but in a chaotic crazy manner bobbing like complex corks upon the heaving sea. Then began the manual transfer of the many trays of fish. The keen eyes

of the Driftermen would observe the movement of the sea and the vessel and at the appropriate moment, as the rowing boat rose above the vessel's side, a tray would be slipped across in neat transfer, as quick as you like! The film is invaluable in capturing this precarious system.

As the fleet fished the Dogger Bank amongst its company, of necessity, was included a Hospital Ship; for as quick-witted and skilled in seacraft as no doubt the driftermen were, the equipment, methods of operating it and the conditions combined to create a most hazardous environment. For example in the transferring of the trays aforementioned, it was not uncommon for a drifterman to lose an arm or to have it badly crushed between the vessel and his own boat.

Not surprisingly the extreme difficulties encountered by the fishing fleets gave rise to an increased sense of community and one of the outworkings from this I learned recently as I looked in a book on British Fishing. In fact it was before the days of the steam drifters back in the more rugged, if that were possible, of sailing drifters. I noticed this photograph of several tenders or rowing boats very similar to the one illustrated on the opposite page, and they were proceeding across the water to a sailing drifter leaning alarmingly in the heavy swell. She was a Mission Ship and the crews were on their way to worship God together — and according to the caption they did so often for as long as three hours or more. Wow, I shouldn't mind guessing that was an amazing time of worship. God stirring their hearts in their adversity; as Proverbs teaches, chapter 20, verse 27, "The lamp of the Lord searches the spirit of the man; it searches out his inmost being."

Imagine the searching out that would have been taking place within the bellies (for this is where a man's spirit is — bang in the centre of his body..... that gut-centre where instinctively and in spite of our head's contrariness, we know something is good and right) of these men as they fished and sailed often violent seas. And the prospect of meeting with like-minded brothers in Christ, voluntarily rowing across to the 'tent of meeting' and then singing praises to God and thanking him for keeping them safe.

There is nothing quite like a company of men together worshipping and praising God. Last night with my brothers in The Norwich Christian Fellowship I did so in the Y.M.C.A. (Saturday, March 12th., 1983) and that word from God by his Spirit about he, with a lamp as it were, searching about our bellies — stirring us to respond; urging us to come out of darkness into his everlasting day.

I can picture that glorious "Ark" upon the Dogger Bank rising and falling upon the turbulent sea. I can see hardy men packed tight together their eyes alight with a love and vivid understanding of the greatness and majesty of God. Their voices bind together and they become one powerful praising voice causing the very ship to reverberate with the strength of their worship. Their marvellous faces, their knarled savagely, work-worn hands are raised up in adoration and true thanksgiving for their saviour's deliverance of their souls and God's heart delights in them.

Great Yarmouth – the medieval town wall by the South East and Blackfriar's towers.
Outside the picture at the right hand side is a plaque upon the remains of Garden Gate which reads:

"In AD 1260 King Henry III gave a charter to the Burgesses of Great Yarmouth conferring upon them the liberty to enclose the town with a wall and moat. The work was commenced in 1284 in the reign of Edward I and completed in 1396. The whole wall was about 2200 yards in length and 23 feet in height. It had 10 gates and 16 towers and enclosed 133 acres. A moat passable by boats was added making the fortress very strong and complete."

By the Garden Gate is a very small, rather neglected Jewish cemetery with about ten tombstones with Hebrew indented lettering standing upon simply dirt or against the walls. God's chosen people, a very special people, praise the Lord that even through holocausts they, by his goodness, have returned to the old Jerusalem.

A little dumb boy got his own pad and pencil
and produced a delightfully symbolic sketch
of the tower with the shed on top.
I saw an old lady whose laceless black shoes
and neglectful state, reminded me of my
childhood and of the poverty I saw around
me in those strangely moving and fascinating
days.

ICTORIA GARDENS

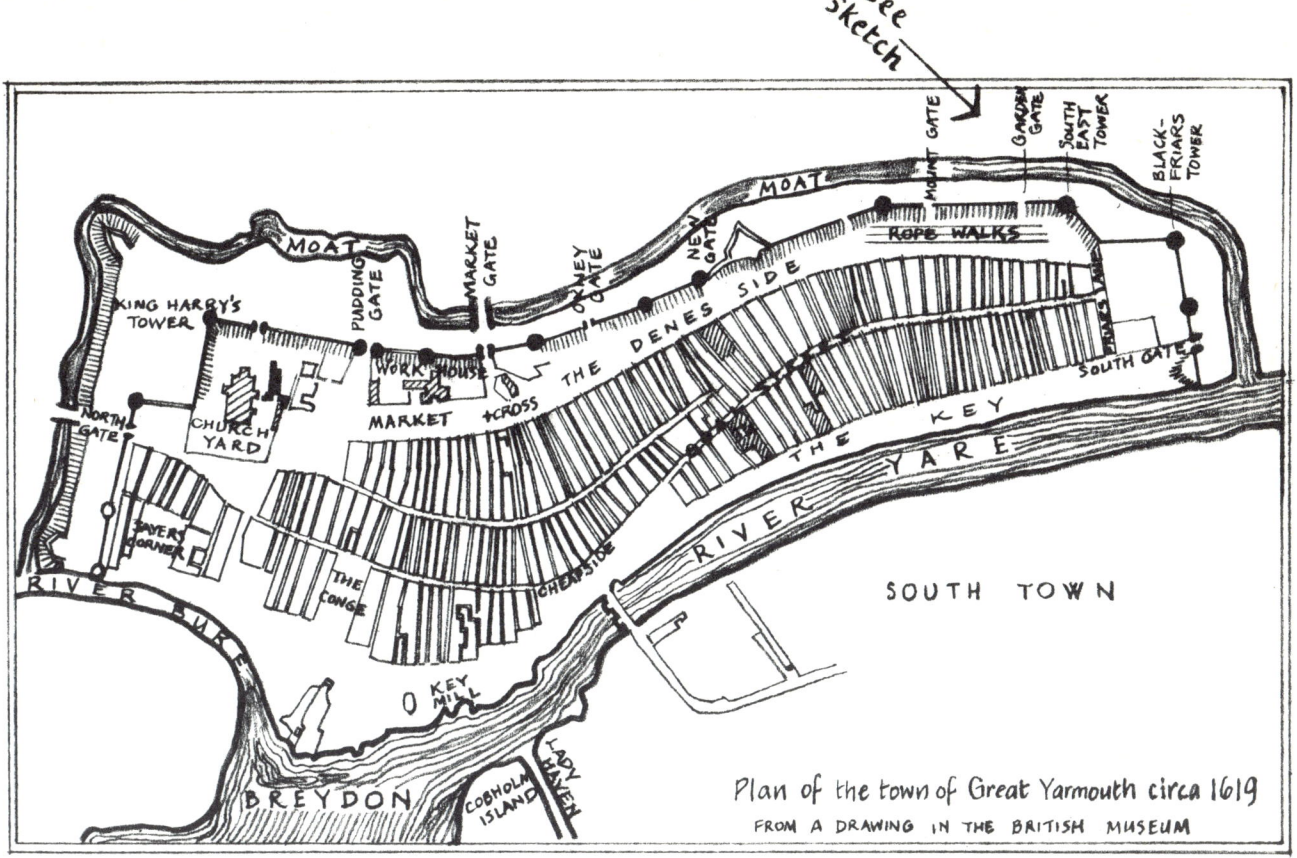

MOAT

KING HARRY'S TOWER

PUDDING GATE

MARKET GATE

ONEY GATE

NEW GATE

MOUNT GATE

GARDEN GATE

SOUTH EAST TOWER

BLACK-FRIARS TOWER

ROPE WALKS

THE DENES SIDE

NORTH GATE

CHURCH YARD

WORK HOUSE

MARKET +CROSS

THE KEY

RIVER YARE

SOUTH GATE

SAYERS CORNER

THE CONGE

CHEAPSIDE

SOUTH TOWN

RIVER BURE

O KEY MILL

LADY HAVEN

BREYDON

COBHOLM ISLAND

Plan of the town of Great Yarmouth circa 1619
FROM A DRAWING IN THE BRITISH MUSEUM

93

Darby's Hard, Gorleston. Times there were when this boatbuilding and repair yard was overwhelmed with work. Charles Darby has retired but in reflecting upon his life, his face lights up as he recalls brimful past days: skippering fishing vessels up and off the East Coast; adzing beautiful wood into shape, apprenticed under his father and then in his own right. "We did just about everything with the adze," he explained. I found Mr. Darby a quiet unassuming man, he and his lovely, faithful wife live quietly in their house just up-river from the old boatyard.